STRESS RELIEVING

WEEEEE BOOK'S

The Blue Book!

Mandalas

Wendy Pikys

Dear artist:

Choose a model that inspires you, select the tools and prepare a quiet place.

If you wish you can play soft music, or light some scented candles or an incense stick.

If you think you need help to exteriorize your emotions, we suggest you color from the inside out.

If you are on an inner quest, for affirmation or self-knowledge, paint from the outside in on the design.

namaste

WEEEEE
BOOK'S

WEEEEE
BOOK'S

WEEEEE
BOOK'S

WEEEEE
BOOK'S

WEEEEE
BOOK'S

We do not see
things as THEY are.
We see things as
WE are.
-ANAIS NAN

WEEEEE
BOOK'S

Your
LIMIT
is
YOU

INHALE
Breathe
EXHALE

WEEEEE
BOOK'S

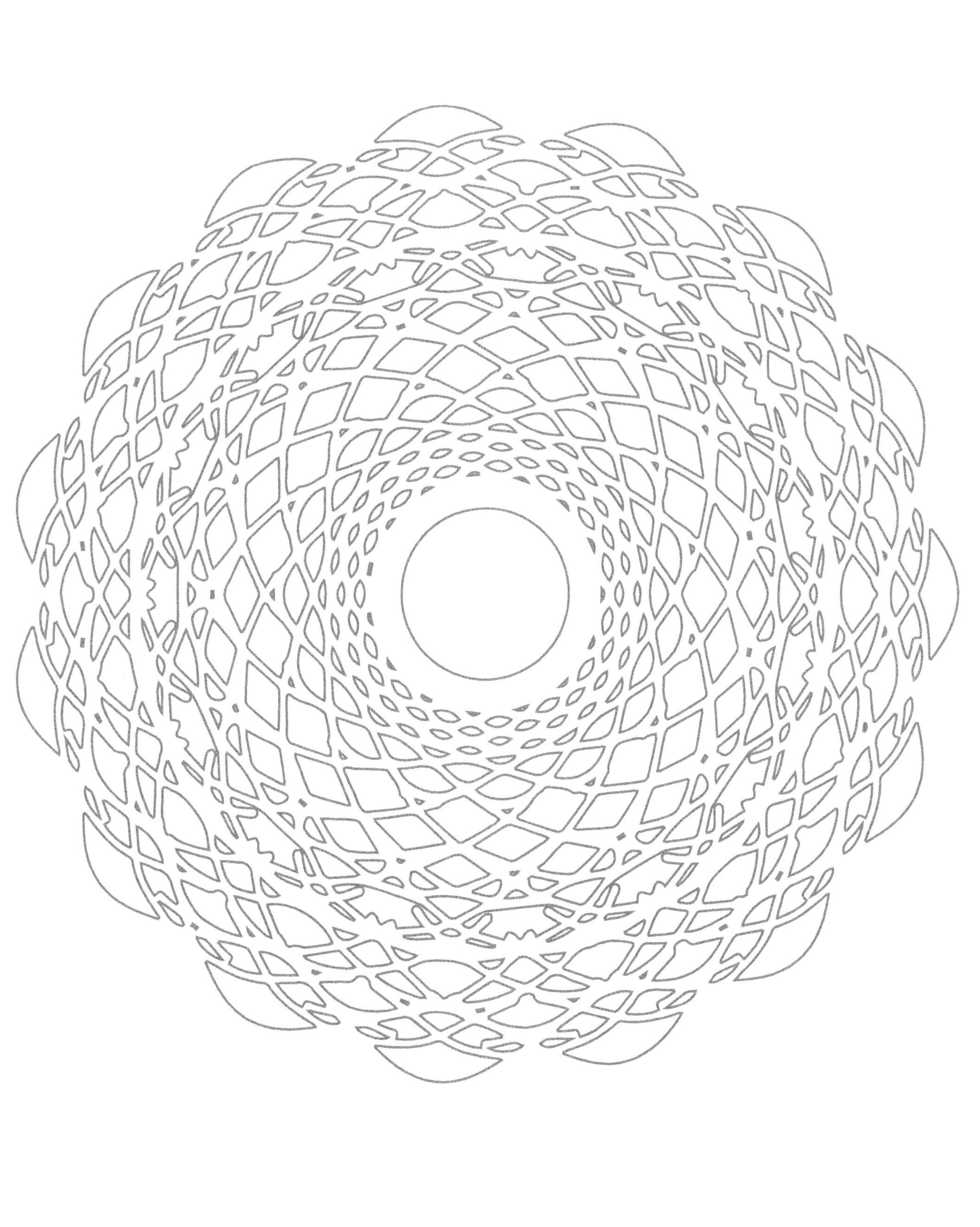

WEEEEE
BOOK'S

Namaste

The Blue Book!

By Wendy Pikys

Mandala is a word of Sanskrit origin and means 'circle'; it represents the unity, harmony and infinity of the universe. It represents the unity, harmony and infinity of the universe.